D1570138

Every Room
We Ever Slept In

Every Room
We Ever Slept In

Jason Shinder

The Sheep Meadow Press
Riverdale-on-Hudson, New York

Cover photograph: From a color original by Joel Meyerowitz

Stanzas from the poem "The Final Soliloquy of the Interior Paramour" are reprinted from *The Collected Poems of Wallace Stevens*. Copyright © 1954 by Wallace Stevens. Reprinted with the permission of Random House, Inc.

All inquiries and permission requests should be addressed to:
The Sheep Meadow Press, Post Office Box 1345,
Riverdale-on-Hudson, New York 10471.

Typeset by The Sheep Meadow Press.
Printed by Capital City Press on acid-free paper in the United States. This book meets the guidelines for permanence and durability of the Committee on Production Guidelines for Book Longevity of the Council on Library Resources.

Library of Congress Cataloging-in-Publication Data

Shinder, Jason, 1955–
        Every room we ever slept in / Jason Shinder.
                p.   cm.
        ISBN 1-878818-05-8
        I. Title.
PS3569.H493E94   1993
811'.54–dc20   93–1243
                                                                           CIP

Distributed by The Sheep Meadow Press.

for my family and friends
and in memory of my father

Out of this same light, out of the central mind,
We make a dwelling in the evening air,
In which being there together is enough

—Wallace Stevens

ACKNOWLEDGMENTS

The poems in this book, or versions thereof, first appeared in the following magazines: AGNI: "Dark Palace," "Crime," "X." *American Poetry Review*: "Good Shepherd." "Once Before The Ocean." *California Quarterly*: "This." *Columbia: A Magazine of Poetry & Prose*: "The Storm, After," *Graham House Review*: "Moviegraphs." *The Kenyon Review*: "The Notebooks of Pablo Picasso." *Michigan Quarterly Review*: "Dedication," "The End." *Mudfish*: "The Pocketbook." *New York Quarterly*: "Two Brooklyn Haikus." *Pequod*: "The Notebooks of Rene Magritte." *Ploughshares*: "Exterior Street, New York City – Night," "Kings Highway," "Work: for Stanley Kunitz." *Provincetown Arts*: "The Notebooks of Salvador Dali." *River Styx*: "Dear Star of Mine." *Shankpainter:* "One Bed."

"Once Before The Ocean" will also appear in the *Fine Arts Work Center Anthology*, 1994.

"The Notebooks of Rene Magritte," "The Storm, After," and "This," also appeared in *Under 35: The New Generation of American Poets*, 1989.

"Boat Knocking" appeared in *A Celebration For Stanley Kunitz*, 1986.

"Prayer" and "The Past" will appear in *Walk on the Wild Side: Urban American Poetry since 1975*, 1993.

The author would like to thank the Fine Arts Work Center in Provincetown, the Yaddo Corporation, and the Michael Karolyi Foundation in Venice, France.

Love and thanks to Steven Bauer, Laurel Blossom, Lucie Brock-Broido, Cornelius Eady, Lawrence Joseph, and Samuel Kashner, for their support and for their help with these poems in manuscript. Deepest gratitude and thanks to Sophie Cabot Black, Stanley Kunitz and Stanley Moss.

"Boat Knocking" is for Catherine Gysin. "Dedication" is for Sophie Cabot Black.

CONTENTS

IV

V

Light the first light of evening, as in a room
In which we rest and, for small reason, think
The world imagined is the ultimate good

—Wallace Stevens

I

WORK

I notice my old love
walking with someone
and I gesture with my glasses
should she recognize me.
I write this line,
fix her safely within it,
and hope my poems appear
in magazines she reads.
As she stands in the kitchen,
stirring her husband's soup,
I hope her eyes fall
on my name, and the terrible
mistake of her life
becomes clear. I will then pray
for a small earthquake.
The cries of the fallen
reach me, and I free everyone
except her. Years later
I find her asleep,
and carry her back to my room
where she remembers nothing
but how I saved her.

CRIME

The trouble with me
        is I don't know
                if I can love a woman.

More than anything I fear
        Mrs. Dreyfuss's lips opening
                to touch mine. How

will I ever kiss a woman
        without ever really knowing
                if it is a kiss?

Her dress is rising. She stops me
        in front of the *Cheerios.*
                How's school?

How's mom? I'm about to confess
        everything: My mother makes breakfast,
                sits watching TV, drinking diet soda –

the soda turns paler, finally
        she falls asleep. She hates
                her dead husband,

her crooked son. But I smile,
        say Mom's fine,
                running for Mayor

as the stolen beer cans hidden
        under my green army jacket
                rub up against my nipples,

wanting to grow breasts of their own,
        large, beautiful as Mrs. Dreyfuss's.
                I hope Mr. Dreyfuss did not see

my eyes moving down the buttons
        of her blouse. I dream
                of circling lazily

around her head, touching
        her hair.
                Although the aisles

are beautiful with candy
        and fruit
                and I love staring

at them, for theirs is a beauty
        of the world
                not human,

I am not thinking about them:
        I am thinking
                about love,

even the reflection of my face
        on the glass
                of the refrigerator of beer

is beginning to tell me
        about it.
                Do not confess:

It is necessary to deny
        everything
                to go on.

MARRIAGE

The woman I marry
will walk into my father's delicatessen,
buy the same tuna and cheese sandwich
she's bought since 1975.
That's how faithful she'll be.
I don't know why
but she'll begin weeping, hair falling
on her shoulders, something
nervously moving through her left hand.
She doesn't want to tell me
but she does. All I do
is sway in and out
of the story she tells,
wondering how long it will take.

MY HANDS

My hands were born naked, blind and pink. My mother held them up to the mirror and gave them names like Right and Left. She dressed them in blue and brown silk, puffed sleeves and sashes. At night they ran away. But when I woke they were beside me. It was strange to bathe and dress them, to watch them hang over the bed like drunk sailors. I made them into stones wrenched from the earth. I made them into clouds drifting away from the body, above the ocean.

As I grew older, I knew my hands less. Their bruises and scratches were their own. I hid them in the deepest folds of my wallet. I made them sleep in pockets, under blankets in stranger's beds. I have lost my hands, I cried.

My mother showed me photographs of my hands as children together, wearing matching gloves – the fair one carrying a tin lunch box, the strong one throwing snowballs.

One night I saw my hands waving across the bay. I swam across the water, opened the hands and stared and stared at them. I held them up to the moon, touching the edge of each finger.

The thought of my hands mine again, the to and fro action of one hand against the other, the way my hands hum, raised me above the ground. I'll be as good as my hands, I said. I'll never let anything they touch go, ever. I'll wash them every morning until they smell like fresh sheets.

Now I am waiting for a son, waiting to properly celebrate my hands moving west to east and back again. It is as if they were playing hide and seek. One looks at me longingly and then disappears behind my back – the other stays in sight, just out of reach, no matter where I reach. Sometimes I am tired as a father who's played all day, some rainy day. Sometimes I don't want to anymore. I don't want to. But my hands keep on playing, so I play.

PLACES HE WASN'T

Just once more I want to hear
the way my father said EHHH
in one breath, his mouth barely opening
after hearing one more story
of how the future was so close,
so far away. It was the slow downward whining
by which his life was given meaning.
Some misery rose in his veins
and the vowels and consonants locked
at the back of his throat.

EHHH. The longing to be places he wasn't.
After the mortgage wolfed down the faces
of the weekly one hundred dollar bills,
after the wheels of his new Lincoln Continental
turned over the same gravelly roads.
Just once more I want to sit beside
him before the turkey and potatoes
and hear his earthly prayer, his poem.

THE POCKETBOOK

My father attacked the steaming pastrami
with a number 7 steak knife for a whiny, lisping woman
who wanted the meat as lean as the white tissue
she took out of her pocketbook, driving her point across
by snapping the purse's rusty brass buckle
shut with all her weight behind it, squeezing
it with her fingers so tight that a piece of skin
broke off and she screamed, as though awakening
in a strange room, as though the Germans had finally
taken Nostrand Avenue and she was caught; naked
the sweat dripping at each pore, the picture
of her parents, the packets of salt and sugar,
the jewelry she had hidden scattered all over the floor.

BOAT KNOCKING

I don't know anything about you, only this:
a studio with one window overlooking the bay

and you are here, a boat knocking in the wind.
You may not like the simile. Especially these days,

you probably think you're the wind. You can be sure
I do too. Sure you're the wind. And what's even more

terrific? You're also the flat sky, beach of this Cape,
and the green stone I picked up for no reason.

They're all the same thing. Only the one lying
outside the heart is safe. But all this is talk,

sleepless, irritable, bull-headed. It's all
or nothing with a blind sadness

for the green in your eyes
when you forget yourself, youthful, the way your hair

falls across your forehead, in the picture
on the wall. I can't tell you

how vivid this feeling is, continuous as waves
washing over everything before I have another chance

to sit with you on the bus. Must I admit I chose
this ending? If ever I had something to say it should

be now, but I can't bring myself to say it or I forget.

THE STORM, AFTER

The telephone poles, upright,
durable, add blue light

to blue light
along the snowy road.

The bay slowly moves
the clouds, the faces

that have carried me sixty miles
into the cut glass of the Atlantic.

The birds are lighter.
And the stones shine. How

do they survive? Two fishermen
slip into a trembling boat.

ONE BED

We lie on one bed,
a lamp at a window,
the darkness of a table and chair.
I can feel with my hand
your stomach rise and fall.
It is so quiet
I wonder if it is the quiet
of our death.
The moon lies on the floor
in the shape of a window,
a bird becomes blank,
perfectly dark.

Now you awaken, your head
nodding from side to side.
You sniff the salty air.
You sense from the corner
of your eye someone there,
someone watching.
You lie down.
I touch your shoulder
and you lean into me
and our bodies enter
every room we ever slept in alone.

II

DARK PALACE

Gables Theater, Merrick, New York

1

A little dark is all it takes.

And then your eyes.

I can talk out loud,
follow you anywhere, look up
at the ceiling,

but I can't find the strength
to touch you...

2

I hold fear over everything,
sea, moon, stars,

the few essential images
in which I almost believe.

3

It used to be I saw you
every so often.

Now every evening I go out
to see what kind of dark it is.

Do not mistake me.

Nothing is clear.

I expect a stone
to open an old sorrow.

4

The moon assails a window
where your bare back
is all I see.

I am not ashamed
to raise my fists
in want of you.

It is only the wind
on your face;
God's breath, God's rough cheek,
that stops me from trembling.

5

I must have lied.

I must have passed the green
of my neighbor's Spruce

once too often
without stopping,

so that what I know
can no longer be sustained.

6

Why isn't your blond hair
beside me?

Is nothing real,

even the diamond
pressed in your hand?

7

I listen to the beating of drums,
enormous stones clashing,
that mouth of yours, those lips.

What was it you said?

I'll go crazy trying to remember.

THIS

I've seen you before:
on a hill, the color of wind,
on a beach, the color of bones.

Where have you been? Nowhere.
I haven't been anywhere. I'm not even here,
but I'm used to that.

You stand so close I inhale your breath.
I tell you everything about my life
because you don't ask.

Maybe you're wearing gloves.
Maybe a hat.
Maybe nothing.

You probably ask, What's kept you?
Perhaps you just stand there, pale
as the ghost the cold leaves in my breath.

You lean over the balcony, above the ocean.
I pull at your sleeve, a beggar
wanting something you don't have.

You might say: The moon is moving the water closer.
You might not.
You turn your eyes toward me.

FLASHBACK

We were wrong all along: the story is here
    inside the light running
all the way down to the sea, the clouds
    moving into another day.

A woman is walking the beach on an island,
    a light breeze parting the hair
on her forehead, a warm August night.
    It happened that day.

A man came from the city to rip
    withered vines from the picket fence
and tell her the news: his silhouette, a bruise
    on the shoreline.

And then the rain staying with her,
    struggling loose from his arms.
Had she turned back she would have seen
    his shadowed figure, hands

over his eyes, shirt unbuttoned, hair
    every which way from a sudden
southern wind. I'm sorry.
    I'm sorry. But she kept on toward

the beach's edge, hands in pockets,
    his face everywhere. Love can crack us
with its fingernail. Look
    how it grins and swings its tail even now.

THE PAST

Along many empty streets my heart is sustained
by the beauty of brownstones

after they are torn down. I still don't know
whether to trust the dead branches,

to rely on broken glass on the sidewalk
made nearly whole again by what it once made visible:

pink and yellow sugary window shades transcending
rotten tin gutters, a passing brown Desoto,

the hand of a young girl in a bright sleeve
dangling from the car window. It is like

my father is alive again, sporting
a well trimmed mustache, his Saturday-night suit.

He is standing in wing-tips in his kitchenette,
sipping tea, scratching tomorrow's beard, scruffy

with romance and sorrow. The light is fading
but I must see him to believe

in the smell of lilacs from across the river.
It is time I put my faith in the past.

It is time I opened the door to his apartment
on 242 Dumont Avenue and confessed everything.

LATE IN THE TWENTIETH CENTURY

It is like the discovery of a new planet,
hidden for eons in the dark,
how the lost appear, sprawled out
on old brown dumps of garbage,

black, rotten mattresses. It is like
watching the farthest stars the way
the lost sleep by calling out the names
of everyone they've never gotten close to.

EXTERIOR STREET, NEW YORK CITY – NIGHT

Someone like The Past walks in,
sits down beside me. The moon blazes
slowly, a burning ship
in its last hour. I try to talk
to the woman inside me
who will not let me sleep.

There is a drink in my hand.
My reflection in the window pane
is small. My face
is the face I have seen
in movies, in the middle
of the night, asking, Where Have I Been?

III

GOOD SHEPHERD

I was on my knees, pulling grapes, filling my basket,
moving on, when I turned my head toward Anna

and became dizzy. When I lifted the basket
from the ground, sat it down on the metal frame

of the tractor, pushed it over with both hands,
I watched the grapes roll down.

I rolled with them. The first morning,
Anna took my hands, showed me how to separate

the grapes from their stems
like a good shepherd. On my hands

the bleeding stopped, began to harden,
go away. Who could say where it all began?

Sienna for Anna? Brooklyn for me? It was something different
for each of us, made us leave home for Paris,

Paris for Bordeaux. Yet it was the same.
Anna had a husband but he left.

I had a friend but he died.
The grapes on the vine were no grapes at all,

but fuzzy, bluish-white ornaments
attached to each other with a sticky substance

of acid and formaldehyde which burned straight-up
in the nostrils and nothing, not the smell

of wild African violets, the rice-chocolates,
or the moon coming into the vineyards,

could make me forget. Two, perhaps, three times, I thought
I had a fever. Anna raised her arms

to wrap a towel round my forehead,
and I leaned forward and smelt the dark,

fluttery grass under her arms.
She always took out two cigarettes, one for her,

one for me, though I never raised a match.
Maybe then I should have invited her to sit

at my father's dinner table. Maybe find her work
as a waitress in one of America's shopping malls,

full of escalators and Muzak. Once she stopped me
walking toward town, offered to trade shoes

and throw in a franc. She gave me the money in advance
and under an orange tree

we deshoed ourselves. Sneakers for her.
Sandals for me. When she pulled

up her green wool socks, she was almost
my sister, her shoulder leaning into mine,

whispering for someone to find her. I held her
whenever I saw her eyes looking back

with only the barest of color.
There are lies. Always. Yes?

Shirt open, cigarette from her mouth.
It's true, I said. How else can we live?

I have this dream, she whispered,
sitting on her cot, speaking of America:

the movies, the song she liked best, *Twist and Shout*.
Could I help her live there too? No.

But a dozen times I said yes. Yes.
We live the same life.

Yet I couldn't imagine anything
for her but staying in the fields, working,

that's all, working, staying in the fields.
I was nineteen. I used to make excuses.

I used to bear the blame. I'll write,
arrange everything. Something can be done.

WAITRESS

There is a table in the back where she opens
her mouth to red lipstick, lets her eyes down
for a touch of blue mascara, and rests

her bunioned feet. Six more hours
before she can sip Coca-Cola and sleep
in front of her father's new Magnavox 14 inch Black & White,

Milton Berle running across the screen.
She touched Mr. Berle's hand once in 1948
when he raised his right arm for her

and a roast beef sandwich. The world shrieked,
rang in promise. She knows it was then the twitching began
in her left eye. Esther is still

waiting tables at Dubrows. Sadie still hanging coats
at Sutters. Sunday, she's got her cousin Lenny's
green Chevrolet. The tall kitchen doors swing back

and forth, parting the hair on her forehead.
She can taste the salt at the back of her throat
thinking of the man

who will lean into her one night. Not the girl
smiling, balancing three bowls of soup on her left arm,
but a woman who would claim all beauty hers,

not to keep it, but to hold it long enough to change.

MY BROTHER

1

My brother, sitting near the fireplace,
is silent. A craftsman
of hammers and wood, I used to think
he was tired of rising,
after so many days with nothing
to build in East Dover, Vermont.

Once a single sheet of paper fell
gently out of his coat pocket.
I read it as he walked ahead;
his thoughts still a secret.

2

Why is he calling from the woods?
I don't know if there will be time
to name and rename the past –
ice that collects along our mouths.

Why does everything drift
through my brother's eyes
the color of the moon, and is gone?

PROVERBS FROM FLATBUSH AVENUE

If you wake up happy it means you cried all night.

If you stand still too long you'll show your age.

When everyone's poor there's no such thing as poverty.

People: they come from everywhere.

The world's a bad fitting and can't be repaired in one sitting.

The sky's too big, the earth's too short.

If you eat the last thing on your plate you'll never be married.

If you say hello you'll have to say goodbye.

Sooner take food from a baby than eat pork.

Death lasts a year at most but suffering is forever.

KINGS HIGHWAY

Just as the car hits the fire hydrant,
the water, smearing its bright load,
blinding the oncoming drivers
who crouch in fear behind their wheels,

a young boy is working the lock
of the glass door of KAPLAN'S JEWELRY STORE
with a pen knife. A Spanish woman,
hiking up the sleeves of her teeshirt,

is speaking against the heat
from her bedroom window: her hair will not dry
before her man arrives. A woman with no shoes
picks up a newspaper from the sidewalk,

lets it drop. A man with a beard is on his knees.
The secret is in the tomatoes. And yet
a woman wearing an apron in front of SY'S GROCERY
is letting them fall through her hands,

remembering only their price. The sky sags
its dumb grey bag of moisture
and heat upon the shoulders of an old man
under The El. Outside FATHER & SON SHOES,

everyone keeps touching the same pair.
The fish in front of RALPH'S SUPERMARKET
shines. A cat alongside HYMIE'S CIGARS
runs with its head down like a tiny buffalo.

MEATIARY

1. Salami

Oily, something whimpers inside.
Always at the point
Of it becoming its own delicacy.
After each slice
The next is smaller,
Troubled.

2. Turkey

Fat bellying out over
Its trousers. It takes four men
To hold it down.
It's about to jump,
Even with a bad back
The moment it realizes it ate
To be eaten.

3. Corned Beef

Lean, still accustomed to life,
Glowing with a baby's pink skin.
It waits hours for something it had
And lost, the way a dog waits
For someone to call it
By its real name.

4. Tongue

It waits hours
Before speaking back,
Carries the weight of everything
Not said.

5. Chicken

The skin of an orange
That has spent its life
Waiting in the dark.

6. Roast Beef

Why not just walk, jump, fly
Into it, savory mass of pink flesh,
More juicy minute after minute. Nothing but rose
Down where it spills a little blood.

7. Bologna

Just as I was about to confess
My love,

I had the desire to eat something.

TWO BROOKLYN HAIKUS

Hey, you with the hat,
blue earmuffs. Talkin' ta ya.
Whah? You President?

**

Loose coins feel like stones,
the rain drops bang noisily,
cigarette in mouth.

36

ONCE BEFORE THE OCEAN

I dreamed I was the first man to speak to God.
He leaned over the mountains, oceans and sod.
He said, *We must carve joy out of stones.*
He said, *Fear of love is joy. It leaves no one alone.*

When I wake I see his shadow.
The sun burns with the darkness of every sparrow.
In the middle of a busy street my eyes close.
His spirit shines out of every window.

Angels will wind up my broken parts.
In The Book, a man's good heart
makes his bones open up with wings.
I lower my head on my knees and I sing.

Once I stood before the ocean, God's house.
The quarter-moon was an old man in bed, praying out loud.
My mouth froze around the O in His name,
as if frozen around everyone's pain.

PRAYER

After Jack paces in circles, head down, decides to say
  something to his wife, says nothing,
after Juan no longer eats at the table with his children,
after Gary steals Mrs. Kaufman's six month late welfare
  check,
after Aaron can no longer lay his head on Esther's breast
  without thinking of Samuel's wife,
after Sy works sixteen hours a day seven days a week one
  hundred and thirty, three hundred, five hundred dollars
  a week fifty-two weeks a year fifty-one years and dies
  of a heart attack without ever really talking to his
  son, Harold,
after Paulie flicks his knife like a match before young
  Sarie's eyes,
after the Scaletti brothers attack the last no-good hair
  on Louie's head,
after Rudy opens Fred's mouth and blows out his tongue
  with a firecracker,
after Joseph splashes gasoline on his boss's Cadillac,
after watching the drop of sulfur flare up purple-edged
  on the matchstick,
after tossing the match,
after Safiya watches Quincy put Max's hand in a fire and
  waits for the fire to end,
after Pete pounds the girl's head against the sidewalk
  harder than anyone,
after Lucy's father makes her scratch the strange hairs
  near his groin,
after Harriet leaves her day old child on the steps of
  the movie house,
after Tommy beats his sleepless, irritable son with a
  baseball bat,

after Chuckie does not break down and confess everything,
after Catherine's moment to confess love passes,
after Fannie's disbelief fans out into clusters of weeds,
after Bobbie is drawn so close to murder it holds her
 before she speaks.

IV

MOVIEGRAPHS

1. showing the world

everything is soft and white
this is how creation appears
in THE BIBLE in the first moment
not like masses of gas
and meteors solidifying but as if God
were a magician waving his beard
and in THE GREEN PASTURES da lawd
sits above the clouds black
cigar from his mouth laughing laughing
for all the stupidity
and murder

Cain it turns out slew
Abel in an Irish frenzy
and a cheery Noah
pottered an ark
wearing heavy eye-shadow
got his animals confused
and a handsome Abraham
stood on a hill
uttered the Bible so slow
his son a foot away from him
could not be saved

O Lord will you forgive us
this that every time we pray
we think of Charlton Heston and worse
Raquel Welch smiling winsomely
in a bikini of wild –
beast skins as your angel
did you leave your seat

when they cast Finlay Currie
as your son

or when Rita Hayworth prayed
before a lip-snarling Charles Laughton
and was rewarded with the head
of Alan Badelon on a plate
you probably shrugged
it off all with the quietest i'm
still here i'm still here
yet help us please night
after night the mechanic-turned
movie director Edwin Porter
keeps a slightly overweight white man
in blackface to entertain us
with his weakness and it doesn't
matter how long ago or how long the movie
lasted (12 minutes) it has seared history
with its little thing of
showing the world

2. love like a wolf

for hours (actually 23 seconds)
we watch Joan Crawford's
straight narrow back stroking
her hair sniffing and
smelling it so clean
as if we washed it ourselves when
suddenly she turns
through the corridors of a moving
train side to side
to side as if only the perfect
thing to do was to walk straight up
and breathe the perfume
of one's hair and come to each
step with such purity
why the light nuzzles the cheekbones
she is looking for someone
or she is trying to escape
from someone because she's in the picture
already like the moon the night
she kissed Clark Cable and he strolled off
in a blue suit and tilted his head
a little like a bird off
the side of the road off camera
so you could continue your journey
always always Samuel Goldwyn said finding
the man was always the last scene love like a wolf
till the very end

3. so here now

was Bette Davis Saturday Afternoon
close up champagne glass pop-eyes popping
we caught the world in a lie
for here after all was a Movie Star
and she was ugly exactly the same as the drunk
woman stumbling up 10th Avenue YOU SEE YOU
SEE she is uglier the dead-white greenish skin
something crawling under a rock the intelligence
of a wide forehead the slowness of lips
moving through disease-infested swamps
with her loyal servant
in JEZEBEL she murders with one stare
in John Huston's IN THIS OUR LIFE
panic and pounding terror we can't talk
GIVE US MORE OF IT we wish to become experts
on fear it throbs to the surface look
from a hospital bed she murders another with her
eyes and a young man takes the fall
in TWENTY THOUSAND YEARS TO SING SING
in his arms Davis cries cries and cries
nothing ever is going to happen
to her he says and she will never get
over it

4. writing history with lightning

remember clearly deciding not to see
the record-breaking one-hundred thousand dollar
spectacle D.W. Griffith's BIRTH OF A NATION
anymore myself this out of sheer
protest

but it is full of rapid-fired split-screened
grandeur not yet surpassed even President Woodrow Wilson
exclaiming after a White House showing "It's like writing
history with lightning!"

and hey feel the breeze that threw
Pet Sister Cameron off the cliffs
into "the opal gates of death" fleeing from
salivating renegade Gus
knowing how clear black his eyes were close

what she feared half-life from went out when
Thomas Alva Edison coaxed black boys to play
"interesting side effects" in TEN PICKANINNIES
nameless children romping as coons snowballs bad
chillun off a dull harmless filter
in his mind

but THE BIRTH OF A NATION
every image is black spot flashes
on long white tubes forever stiffening the body
with "hatred so jealous of life" Lillian Gish said
"We were rehearsing the scene
where the colored man picks up
the Northern girl, gorilla-fashion, my hair,

which was very blond, fell far below my waist
and Griffith, seeing the contrast in the two figures,
assigned me to play Elsie Stoneman"

and then out of everywhere the last scene a white day
of KKK out wearing sheets
to stop black impish intents who "rape and
crush the white South after the Civil War"
Bang Bang you're dead I Shoot You Like That
Toss My Cape drink the wine true
defenders of family honor till the next
dark up movie baaaddd niggers
the final final scene brilliantly lit superbly edited
decades later James Earl Ray "sitting pure in his cell"

5. making a difference

keep watching George Bailey
in the last scene of IT'S
A WONDERFUL LIFE stare moon-faced daddy-up
grateful for his family friends no
bitter questions to catch the vague
doubtful air of existence no man
is a failure who has friends
these words running in his head light-happy
a half-mile up from the coast
of his sadness starred with holes when
love broke dreams dived seaward
their red bricks now christmas lies
golden on Bedford Falls Every Life Is
Important Because It Touches So Many
Other Lives "the most satisfying message"
James Agee wrote keep
watching remembering almost everyone
in the movie is dead George Bailey's
brother Harry his wife Mary
just a few years ago I
think of my own life thirty years from now
wonder if I'll be grateful as George
trying to remember how each of us
are necessary banker salesman poet
changing so much all the time ordinary
gestures keeping on just being
here all of us being here helpless
making a difference

6. our song

I've got no love to keep me warm
is from a song
and it works underground in the streets of
Manhattan in ON THE AVENUE
when Alice Faye
overcomes the bones
of all her pain
winded and rained upon
nothing grows a whole
life's love like the beauty
of a popular song that longs
to be tenderly alone
with no one but Fred Astaire black
hat black tie white piano
ballroom lighted by one woman
who adores him

romance is not a flower romance
is a song sophisticated witty
polished lightly rising above
The Great Depression poor rural
whites urban blacks
but then we were never protest
blues singers in '33
speeded-up talkers waterers
of the soul tunnel-shooters of
fear sprouting the loveful Cole Porter line
when we begin the beguine
let the stars that were there before
return above you till

you whisper to me once more, Darling
I love you

forgetting World War II The Big One wafting March
to December and oh all the time
we don't know someone
yet and the years so full of poverty
scalding blankness we crave song
more than first-hand present

oh you can keep the serious
in far countries
Mozart and Beethoven with symphonies
in their hair but
us young us old us twenty
with an Irving Berlin song
Lady, listen to the rhythm
of my heartbeat, and you'll
know just what I mean. Embrace me,
my sweet embraceable
you, a masterpiece

but such a cliché
and on a cheap radio but
nevermind the future high-life
mongers breaking down popular songs
to popular feelings
the sometimes tinkling syncopated
pieces of thin
music is not thinness of soul

but reminders of How Good It Felt
When We Met
or See How Good It Feels
Again Now
this moment yellow and ruffled
whiffled through with promise

7. 1939

enthralled with not knowing and then
the Arizona skyline in STAGECOACH
black and white sun silhouetting Monument
Valley not a path untouched
white-stone treeless hills rising at dawn we
practically forget we love life
too little it's like someone
beautiful is going to walk in change
the south face of Europe close down
troops storming into Poland listen
streams of *Rhapsody in Blue* swell
over snow-covered avenues in MIDNIGHT
the Brooklyn Bridge spreadeagle
to four corners of the earth newsreels
half-burning missed or missing evidence
of soldiers we sink into the velvet-skinned
seats into another seat another evening
left hand round cool liquor of Coca-
Cola right hand round bucket of pop-
corn how is it Scarlett O'Hara
in GONE WITH THE WIND walks full-grown
from a thousand hillsides among the pale
face Confederates dying in Atlanta when
she takes off her sweater we think
she will take off everything oh
we want the rest of our lives to be
the patriotic fervor of Senator Smith
in MR. SMITH GOES TO WASHINGTON does it
matter history is a blur in
YOUNG MR. LINCOLN

Clark Gable Greta Garbo Hattie McDaniel
Jean Harlow Shirley Temple Marlene Dietrich
Barbara Stanwyck Nina McKinney Paul Robeson
so majestic lit up Louis B. Mayer
Samuel Goldwyn Adolf Zuker Harry Cohen
Cecil B. DeMille so powerful half the electrical
world has a movie house in each town look
you can see people on line waiting
for anything anything larger faces
sloping upward beauty-minded songs
by Dorothy in THE WIZARD OF OZ
reveled in technicolor her eyes up cheek
petals red lush song-words lifting
the wind oh Dorothy can melt chairs with
the blue-hearted lullaby "Over the Rainbow" why
aren't our lives changed

Dear Star of Mine:

It was love that made me break the antenna of your car where only last week I attached a pink rose. Where are you? You haven't returned my phone calls. I was always good at convincing myself what you did was because you were so beautiful. But tonight I waited on your doorstep. I need to know if you love me or not. It's not your love, really, I doubt. But how you think about it. I know you love me. Remember how you longed for Mrs. Albert in *After The Rain* before seeing her every night? You were sweet, earnest, and your kisses were always good. There's just a charm and assurance in your love-making my husband doesn't have. Well, sometimes your love feels too headstrong, like in that movie where you got dressed and left the apartment of that young girl while she was still sleeping. It's 3 AM. Where are you? You're always running away from someone you love. You keep traveling from one side of the world to the other, and back again, dragging your passion for me!

real love,

Dolores

X

My life has been this terrible thing
inside of me
and I imagine nothing that might

help it save perhaps another flick,
a truly amazing Flat Four
with the precise architecture

of a woman's breasts hanging
just above the navel. Lately,
I've been watching

young women on their knees
ripping open zippers,
hair flapping against their cheeks,

yellow teeth shining beneath
a fly swinging
on a single light bulb

in the corner of a room inside a room
at the end of a hall. And then
the kiss that makes men cry.

THE END

Always I am afraid
of this moment:
of the return to light.

Words passing from mouth
to mouth
as people follow the Exit Signs.

How did the movie star
holding the beautiful brunette
in his arms

become two men talking Spanish?

V

DEDICATION

When you look back it is still awful,
but also beautiful. Nothing is smooth.
The light is always rough,

anxious. But for the stubborn fact
we imagine things will be clearer
we go on. The angels, for whom we work,

will let us into paradise, say
look, that's all, a mist
you cannot see as long as you are in it.

LIVES OF THE ROMANTICS

1. *The Notebooks Of Rene Magritte*

I

I found myself alone in the middle of the night and discovered my mother was gone. Noticing footprints on the steps, I followed these to the bridge over the local river. My mother had thrown herself into the water. When I fished out her body, her face was covered by her nightgown. How proud, I felt, being the pitiful center of a tragedy.

II

The bell rings. It's my wife's lover. He introduces himself, as if we hadn't met. He is highly respectable, bourgeois. I invite him in, step back to let him pass and, the moment he sets foot in the drawing room, give him a tremendous kick up the backside. He hesitates between the multitude of reactions that come to mind. In the end he sits down, as if nothing happened, on the chair, which I, as if nothing happened, hasten to offer him.

III

One night I shared a room with a bird asleep in a cage. I woke up and, by some glorious delusion, saw, instead of a bird, an egg inside the cage.

IV

A little girl and I climbed an old disused cemetery of a provincial town. We explored the vaults whose heavy trap doors the wind lifted. When we climbed up again into daylight, the columns were broken and scattered among the dead leaves.

V

Lying on the beach is a mermaid whose top half is of a fish, and whose bottom half is the belly and legs of a woman.

VI

In front of a window seen from inside a room I placed a picture representing exactly that part of the landscape which was covered by the picture. The tree in the picture represented the tree standing behind it, outside the room.

VII

A woman on a bicycle brushed past me, accompanied by a man, also on a bicycle. It was night, and I clearly saw the woman move away, her stockings white, and I was still very much aware of her after she disappeared around the corner.

VIII

The problem of the door is finding the opening. The problem of the rain is finding the great clouds which creep over the ground.

IX

I watched someone unroll a length of blue silk and the silk frightened me. I was afraid to come near it. Yet there was nothing threatening about it. The person showing it to me and smiling barely paid attention to it. At that moment, I became aware of where I was. I was on a Pacific Island, and there were women clinging to my sides, faces to the ground, not daring to look at this piece of silk they were seeing for the first time.

X

The first feeling I remember is when I was in a cradle, and the first thing I saw was a chest of drawers next to the cradle. The world presented itself in the guise of a chest.

2. *The Notebooks of Salvador Dali*

I

I pushed a beautiful, curly-headed, little blond playmate off into space as I was helping him along on his tricycle. Going over a bridge that had no railing, and having made sure no one could see us, I shoved him off a bridge of several meters, down on the rocks below. Pretending to be heart-broken, I ran home to get help. He was bleeding profusely. The whole house was in an uproar. I sat in my little rocking chair, rocking back and forth, snacking on grapes and watching the feverish commotion of the adults, enjoying the peaceful darkness in my corner of the sitting room.

II

I love to crack the skulls of birds between my teeth. I regret only that I haven't gotten to eat a famous turkey, cooked alive, which is, it is said, a magical dish.

III

I want to make a book of color illustrations that would make it impossible for men to go to bed with women. I want to sign a contract to put up with pain forever. I want to melt the heavy, oak grandfather's clock in the sitting room, and hang it in the closet.

IV

I got down on all fours and swung my head left and right until
it was gorged with blood and I became dizzy. With my eyes
wide open, I could see a world that was solid black, suddenly
spotted by bright circles that gradually turned eggs fried
sunnyside down.

V

I was walking with my mother and sister in the snow, which I
was experiencing for the first time. I floated on a magic carpet
that crackled lightly under my steps. Soon I was floating in a
forest, and suddenly I stopped: in the middle of a clearing,
something was there in the snow, waiting for me. It was a
plain tree pod, slightly split so as to reveal the fuzz inside. A
single ray of sun, sneaking through the clouds, hit the
yellowish fuzz like a tiny projector and brought it to life. I
rushed toward it, kneeled down and, with all the care one
could take, picked it up, a wounded bird, and cupped it to my
hands. I brought my lips near it and kissed it. I took my
handkerchief and wrapped it up. I told my sister and mother
that I found a dwarf monkey, and my only desire was to show
it to the girl waiting for me by the fountain.

VI

I saw huge phosphorescent eggs like the cold expressionless eyes of a gigantic animal with slightly bluish white eyeballs.

VII

I took off my trousers and poured a sack of kernels on me to form a big pile on my belly and thighs. I wallowed in the enjoyment of the corn, heated by the burning sun, the prickling of the kernels against my skin.

VIII

I was dining with Laura. At the end of the table were champagne bottles, and rare and precious bottles of wine. I was at the end, gazing at them. Laura was in an armchair, reading the newspaper. Suddenly, the maid, going through the room exited with a loud slamming of the door. One of the bottles was shaken and began to roll past me from the other end of the table. It fell on the floor with a great noise, a wondrous ejaculation. Laura looked up from reading the newspaper, stared at me. Meanwhile another bottle, and another, and another, under the same impetus, started to roll.

IX

This evening I went into the garden and bit just once into each of the vegetables and fruits: onion, beet, melon, plum. I felt a little of their juices run into my mouth, through the wounds made by my teeth, and even gnawed on the plum like a vampire drawing his strength.

X

Lying on the balcony, I watched the foaming waves in the sky, as they went by through the brilliant light. Breasts, buttocks, heads, horses, elephants, clocks, crosses paraded before my eyes. I was a witness to monstrous couplings, titanic struggles, tumults and gatherings of crowds. All the phantasmagoria of my childhood came back to my life at my command.

3. The Notebooks of Vincent Van Gogh

I

I got up at six o'clock. I went downstairs to the kitchen. My mother appeared in the doorway, dressed in blue shorts, holding a mirror up toward the light. She looked so tired from work, thin and young, hardly more than fifteen. I said "hello." She peered blindly for a second into the mirror and said, "halo." After a pause, she asked, "Who am I?" I said, "My mother." She couldn't remember. Then she said, "Do you know where my slippers are?" "What do you mean, where your slippers are?" I answered. I got down on my knees and began feeling around. "I can't find my slippers," she said. "They're on your feet," I said. "You've been wearing them all the time."

II

Knowing you suffer seems to make people warm up to you quicker. They treat you almost as if you were a hero. You should have seen the way Lucinda, who never noticed me, walked up to me after she heard I was sick.

III

The night is more alive, more richly colored than the day. The lanterns of the cafes glow hospitably, townspeople sip drinks, chat and stroll under the stars, which hang like lamps in the royal blue dark.

IV

Those who don't believe in the moon are infidels.

V

"You've become impossible again," my brother said last night. Yesterday, ignoring everyone, I stayed in my room all day. And today I sat by the window staring at the trees, smoking cigarettes. "You're making me crazy," my brother said. Why do I feel so bad for myself? As always, again, I'm wrong. There's no reason for my feelings. There couldn't be. But I can't help it. My body aches. I want a woman. I'm jealous of others.

VI

The sunflower is where the start of each day springs to sight. From it I learn to stoop over and to straighten quickly in the constant line of the horizon which borders on my hand. To see the earth give birth to one sunflower through a slant of light is to no longer hate what I've ceased to love.

VII

Sitting quietly in my room, I heard Karina in the kitchen sit down at the table, wanting to be left alone for some private thought. I listened as she sat for a while, then walked excitedly to the stove, and back to the table again. As I listened, I thought of her breasts. I knew she was wearing a green cotton shirt. I grew anxious about seeing her – then my listening and dreaming about her would be called upon. Surprised and friendly, I later smiled at my strange friend.

VIII

Madness discovers itself in love. Sane, can I ever be satisfied?

IX

The windows went in. The windows went out. The sun washed the walls clean as bones. Someone was knocking. There was an ear in my hand.

X

I took a journey on foot to visit my brother. At a few hundred yards from his house, I entered a farm. I stopped behind a manure pile and shot myself. I did not put the gun to my head or my heart, but against my stomach. Later, my brother discovered me, lying on the floor, face down. He ran for help. The doctor said I would survive. Then I'll have to do it all over again, I said.

4. *The Notebooks Of Pablo Picasso*

I

Before a rendezvous with Margaret in her apartment on the outskirts of Sienna, I dropped by the pharmacy and asked for a condom. When Odette arrived in the middle of the day, I virtually tore off her clothes in front of the opened door. Odette, whose bosoms I cannot stop nuzzling, is wildly jealous of Margaret. Odette lies about her past and present but at the end of several long hours, in which much wine is consumed, I always make love to her from the rear. Oh she is seductive, wildly seductive, and after teasing me a bit she gives in. I give in. Days pass. Or so it seems. When I returned to Margaret I was brighter, better looking, more beautiful. There I painted a nude in a seaside apartment belonging to her ill lover. I stared and stared at her breasts as if love were a single thing.

II

I think of betrayal the moment I think of pleasure.

III

"There is always self-deception," Louise told me last night, shirt open, cigarette from her mouth. It's true, I thought. When I met her she was making dreadful lamps out of neon tubing in Paris, living with an architect named Remi. We became so close to being happy, I refused to sleep with her anymore. Instead, I rented her a flat to provide the solitude she needed to paint and, more importantly, so she wouldn't wake up next to Remi. "Painting is good for the circulation," she says. She is a skinny, angular beauty, with deep-set, brown, elegantly lidded eyes that express determination, foolishness, intelligence, gaiety and sadness. I painted her head in brown squares with sincerity, thoroughly, but utterly wrong. Today we rose and made love before breakfast. "I had this dream," she told me.

IV

The one thing I have over angels is I have to sing out of adversity. I challenge the savior to come down with his despair.

V

Dark, and then suddenly yesterday the green eyes of a seated woman drew the stars out of the sky, her arms and legs floated, rocked sideways, through wind, through rain; astonishing in their trembling, their nervousness, their wetness. Her breasts appeared in mist, the distance between two shores, with the color of oranges. Her nose balanced the earth on its stem.

VI

I'm tired of having to paint to get attention.

VII

What is happening? Some accident? Oh are the guns out
again? Is France in danger? I'll lift my brush to canvas until
half the people are covered in a blue light.

VIII

Last night I dreamed a woman was standing beside the
window, naked, her body strangely new and beautiful, and
then she turned and faded or I turned and faded. In any case,
there was a delirious war in her dreaming self, a war of tears,
unable to admit her need for someone, for the strength it
would take to love someone back, as she stood by the window,
listening.

IX

Today my teenage daughter turned her lopsided head, her
stony eyes, toward her tall boyfriend.

X

To put it in black and white: if God could he'd whisper to us
not to fear. But it isn't worth it. And besides, there are words
even God can't say, not even to his son.

WORK

for Stanley Kunitz

Poem is difficult when it's still dark,
lying in bed without sleep.
Poem is difficult entering the kitchen,
another working day.
The poem I once loved made breakfast
while I wrote down my dreams.
I remember the first poem, brown hair piled high
above a never-to-be nordic smile,
a crown of lit candles and leaves.
When I mentioned the word love, keeping it on my tongue,
poem said, yes, yes, love,
but neither of us really knew.
I swore never to hurry poem, never say,
What time is it? Are you ready?
I played Frank Sinatra singing
the summer wind came blowin' in,
a glass of wine on the table.
I wore nothing under a black, silk robe,
read poem the great poets.
Where is the poem of June 6, 1975,
sitting before the window of my father's house?
Poem dressed in purple with the promise of Spring.
Poem of the moon dreaming in its October night.
Let's face it. Poem loves me
but doesn't love me enough.
Poem just wants to be adored,
swinging from bar to bar, eighteen years old.
Maybe poem will be the light I need.
Maybe it's dark inside the body no matter how bright poem.
Maybe we'll marry. Maybe we won't. No matter.
Poem is a window open and a faint breeze.

NOTE:

JASON SHINDER was born in 1955 in Brooklyn, New York. He has a novel, *Liars* in the works. He is the founder of the Writer's Voice of the West Side YMCA and founder and executive director of the National Writer's Voice Project of the YMCA of the USA.

Educated at Skidmore College and the University of California at Davis, he has held fellowships from the Fine Arts Work Center, Naropa Institute and the California Artists Foundation. He has taught at the Guggenheim Museum and the University of California at Davis and currently teaches at the New School for Social Research.

Jason Shinder edited *Divided Light: Father and Son Poems*, an anthology published by the Sheep Meadow Press in 1986. His other anthologies include: *First Light: Mother and Son Poems* (1991) and *More Light: Father and Daughter Poems (1993)* both published by Harcourt Brace Jovanovich.

The Ecco Press is offering a series of cassettes of Shinder interviewing various poets on poets: *The Essential William Blake with Stanley Kunitz, The Essential Lord Byron with Paul Muldoon, The Essential John Donne with Amy Clampitt, The Essential John Keats with Philip Levine, The Essential Wyatt with W.S. Merwin.*

He manages his time between New York City and Provincetown, Massachusetts.

Poetry from The Sheep Meadow Press

Desire for White
Allen Afterman (1991)

Early Poems
Yehuda Amichai (1983)

Travels
Yehuda Amichai (1986)

**Poems of Jerusalem
and Love Poems**
Yehuda Amichai (1992)

Father Fisheye
Peter Balakian (1979)

Sad Days of Light
Peter Balakian (1983)

Reply from Wilderness Island
Peter Balakian (1988)

5 A.M. in Beijing
Willis Barnstone (1987)

Wheat Among Bones
Mary Baron (1979)

The Secrets of the Tribe
Chana Bloch (1980)

The Past Keeps Changing
Chana Bloch (1992)

Memories of Love
Bohdan Boychuk (1989)

Brothers, I Loved You All
Hayden Carruth (1978)

Orchard Lamps
Ivan Drach (1978)

A Full Heart
Edward Field (1977)

Stars in My Eyes
Edward Field (1978)

New and Selected Poems
Edward Field (1987)

Embodiment
Arthur Gregor (1982)

Secret Citizen
Arthur Gregor (1989)

Nightwords
Samuel Hazo (1987)

Leaving the Door Open
David Ignatow (1984)

The Flaw
Yaedi Ignatow (1983)

The Ice Lizard
Judith Johnson (1992)

The Roman Quarry
David Jones (1981)

Claims
Shirley Kaufman (1984)

Summers of Vietnam
Mary Kinzie (1990)

The Wellfleet Whale
Stanley Kunitz (1983)

The Moonlit Upper
Deckerina
Naomi Lazard (1977)

The Savantasse of
Montparnasse
Allen Mandelbaum (1987)

Ovid in Sicily
Ovid-translated by
Allen Mandelbaum (1986)

Aerial View of Louisiana
Cleopatra Mathis (1979)

The Bottom Land
Cleopatra Mathis (1983)

The Center for Cold Weather
Cleopatra Mathis (1989)

About Love
John Montague (1993)

To Hold in My Hand
Hilda Morley (1983)

A Quarter Turn
Debra Nystrom (1991)

The Keeper of Sheep
Fernando Pessoa (1986)

Collected Poems: 1935-1992
F. T. Prince (1993)

Dress of Fire
Dahlia Ravikovitch (1978)

The Window
Dahlia Ravikovitch (1989)

Whispering to Fool the Wind
Alberto Ríos (1982)

Five Indiscretions
Alberto Ríos (1985)

The Lime Orchard Woman
Alberto Ríos (1988)

Taps for Space
Aaron Rosen (1980)

Traces
Aaron Rosen (1991)

Other Titles from The Sheep Meadow Press

— NOTES —

DATE DUE